CLAIRE BRETECHER

More Frustration

*TRANSLATED FROM THE FRENCH
BY ANGELA MASON AND PAT FOGARTY*

METHUEN · LONDON

First published in Great Britain by Claire Bretecher and distributed
by Methuen London Ltd., 11 New Fetter Lane. London E C4P 4EE.

ISBN: 0413 53760 9

PRINTED IN SPAIN

AMAZON

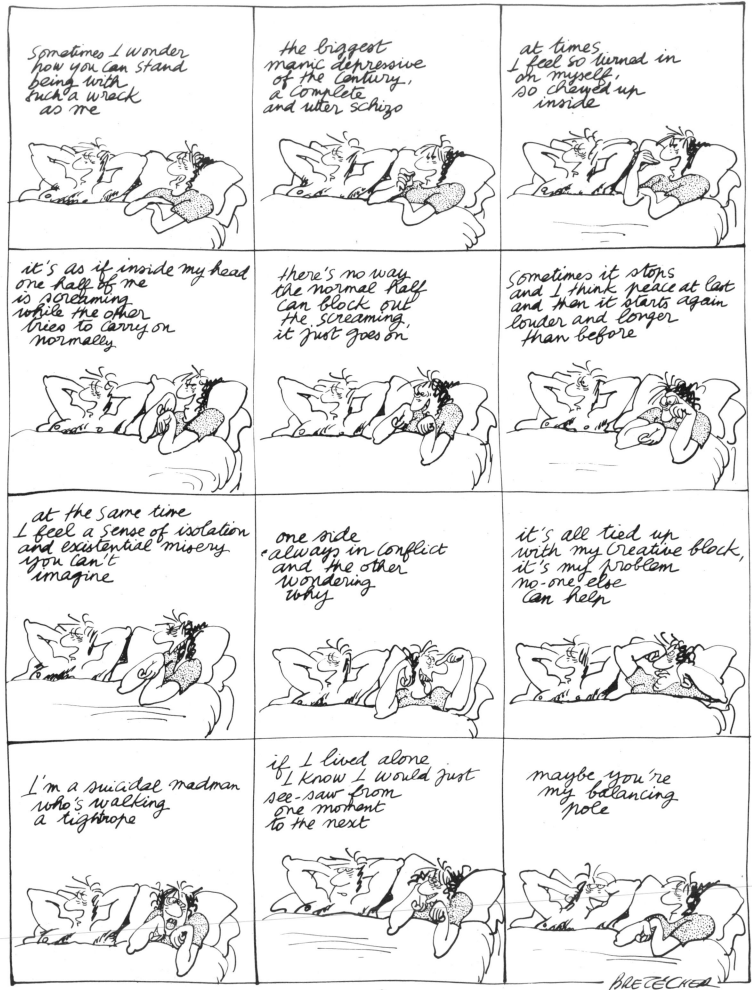

ART APPRECIATION

ALL IN THE MIND

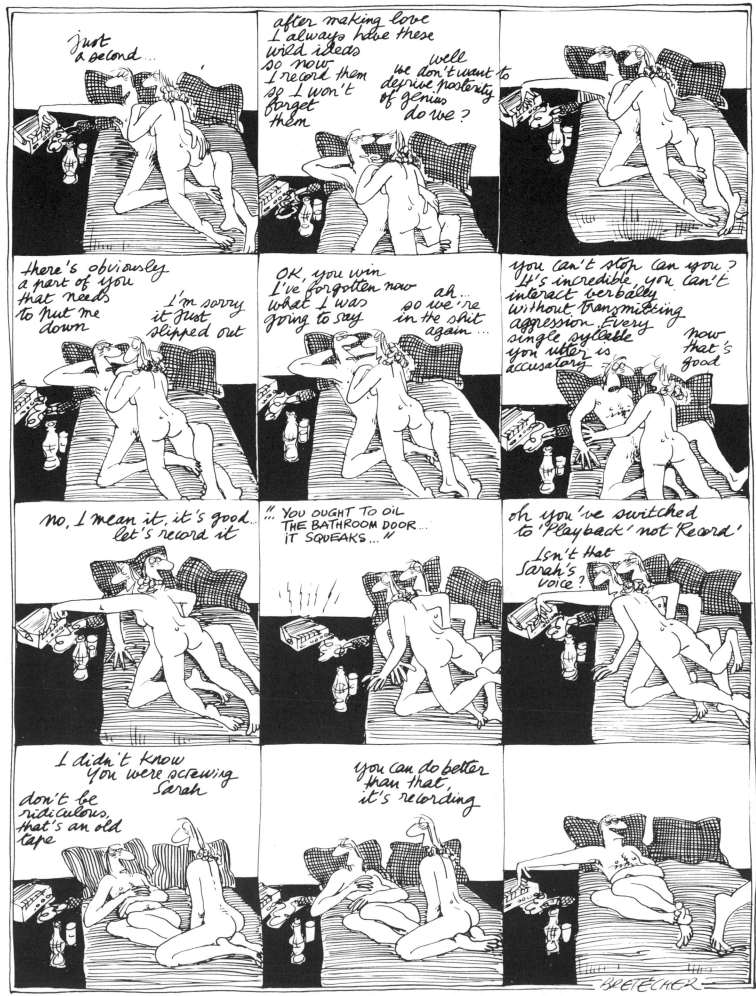

THE SUCKERS

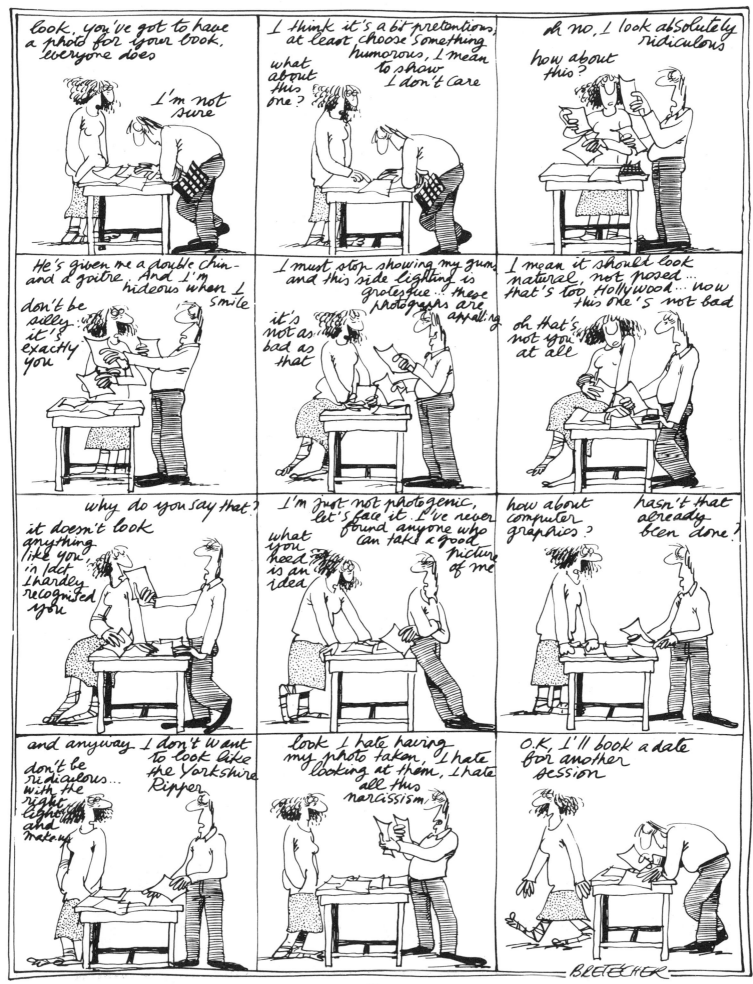

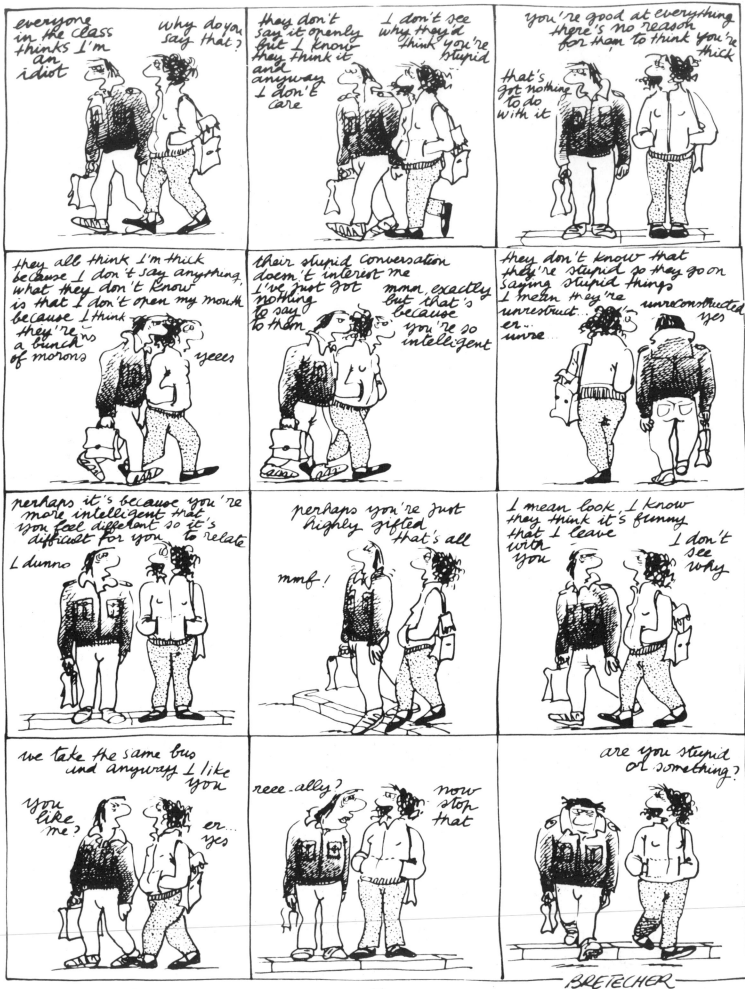

BRETECHER

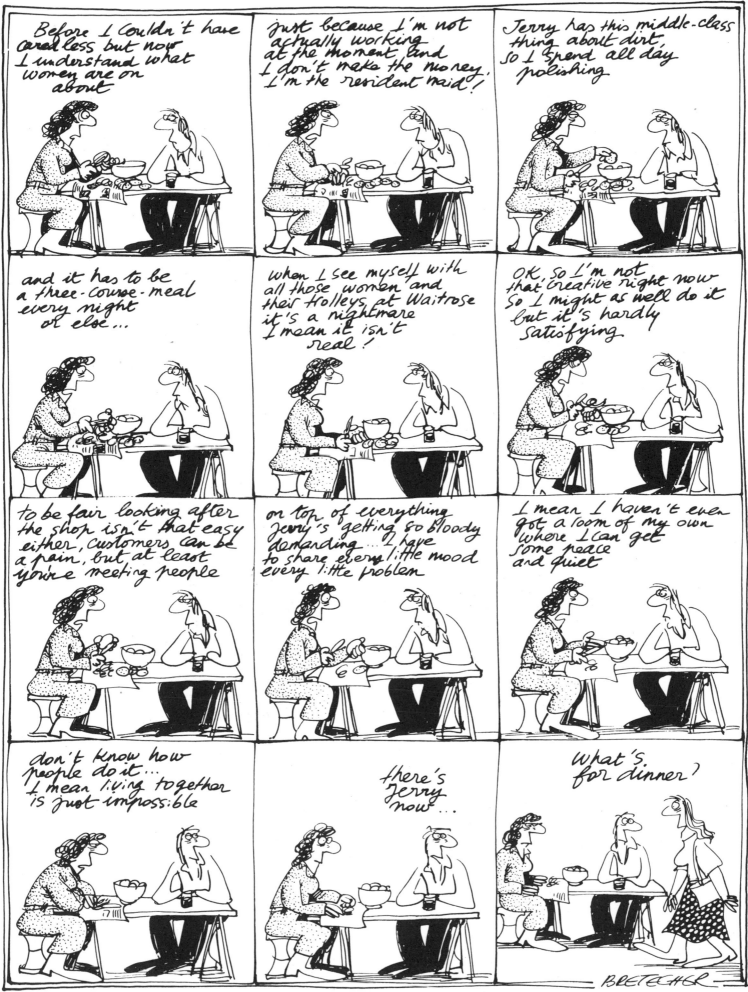

THE WAY OF ALL FLESH

BIG GIRL

oh it's Penelope isn't it? What a big girl we are!
we remember Mrs Hall, granny's neighbour, don't we?
what do we say to Mrs Hall?
Come now, granny taught us how to say "how do you do" properly didn't she?
if you say hello nicely Mrs Hall will give you...
...a nice acid drop with sherbet on the top
how do you do Mrs Hall...
there's a good girl
what one goes through for a fix!
BRETECHER

DIVORCE

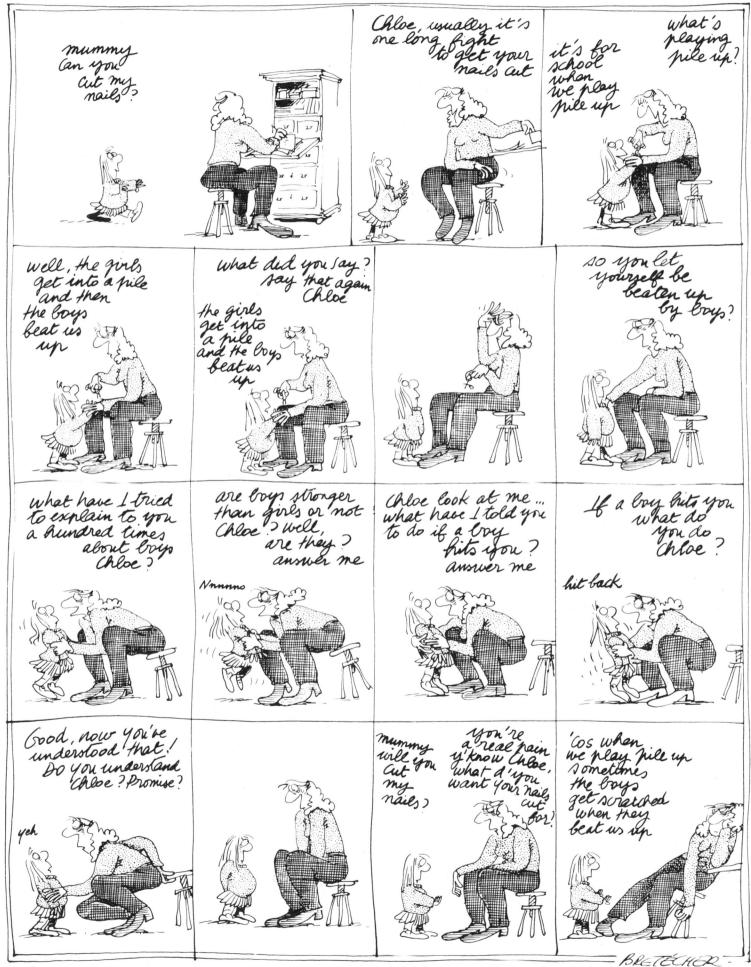

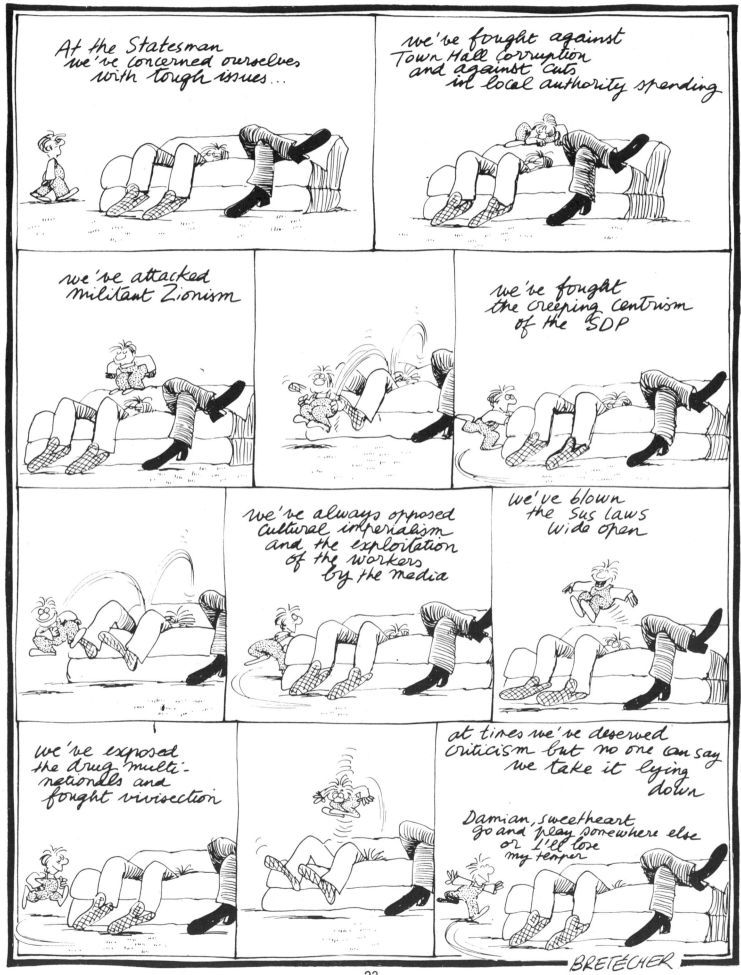

ODE TO TINTIN

BLOOD IS THICKER THAN WATER

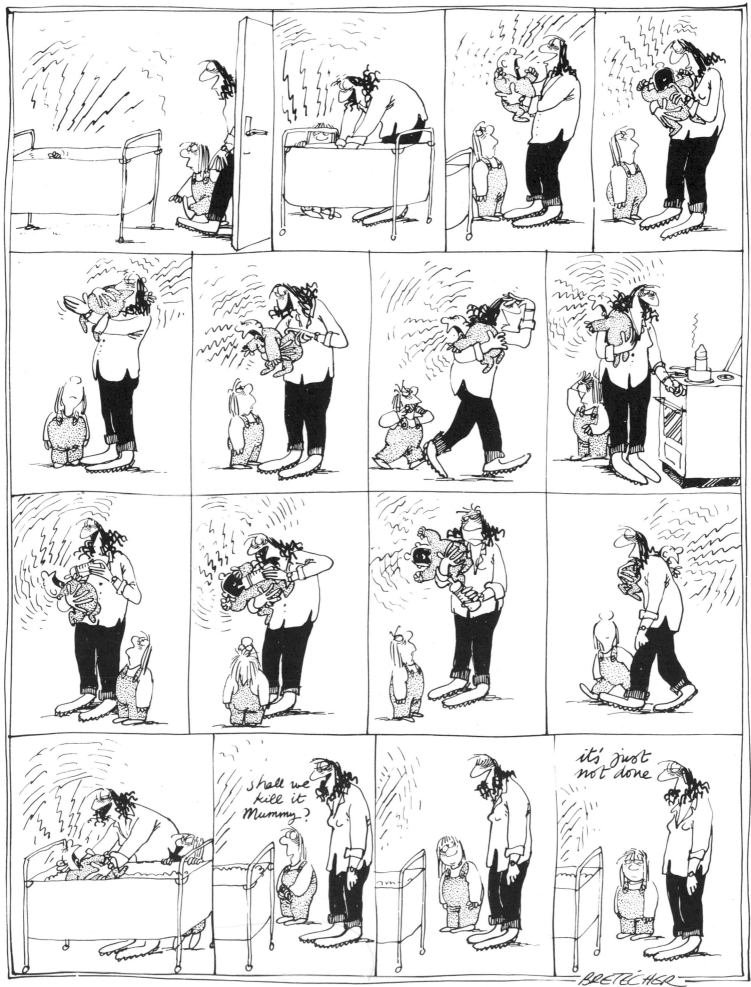

NATURE'S CALL

FIASCO

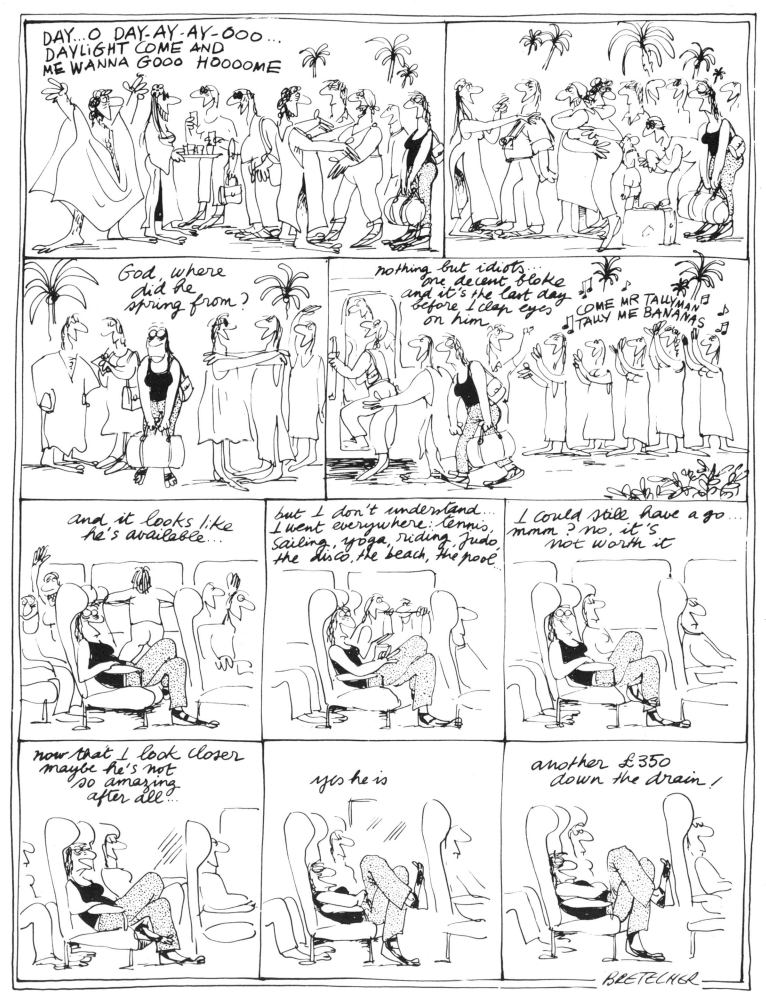

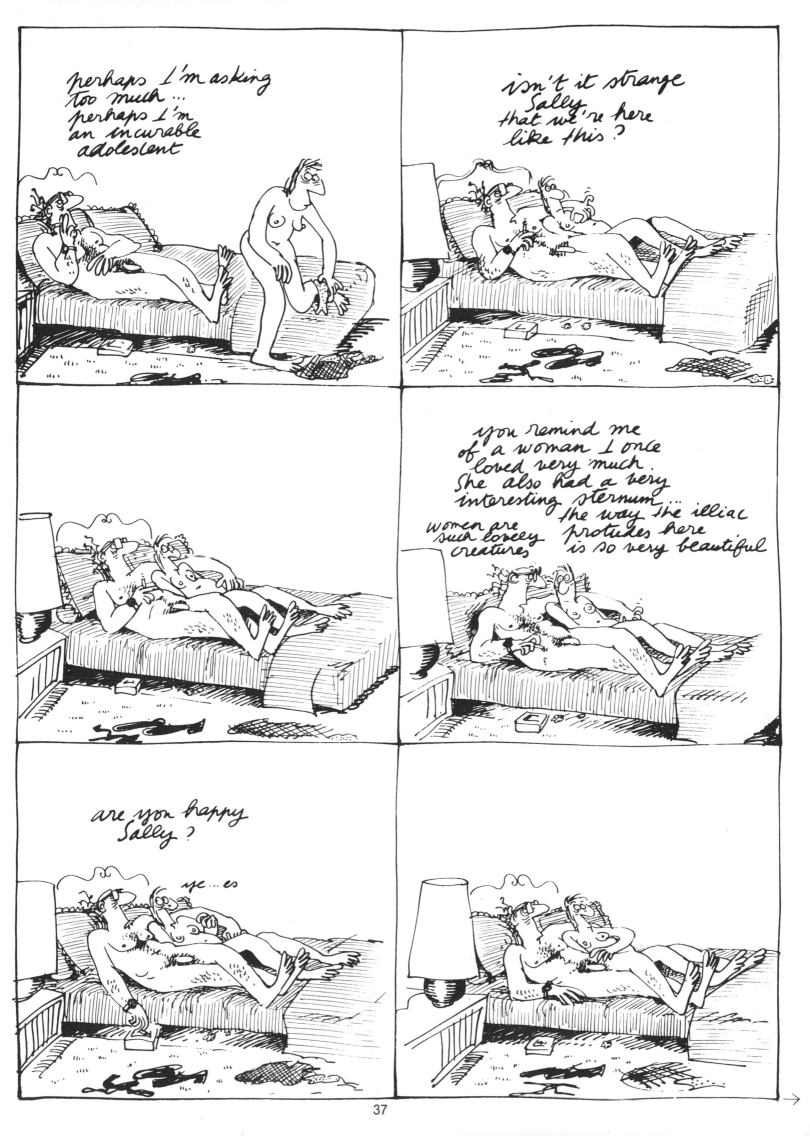

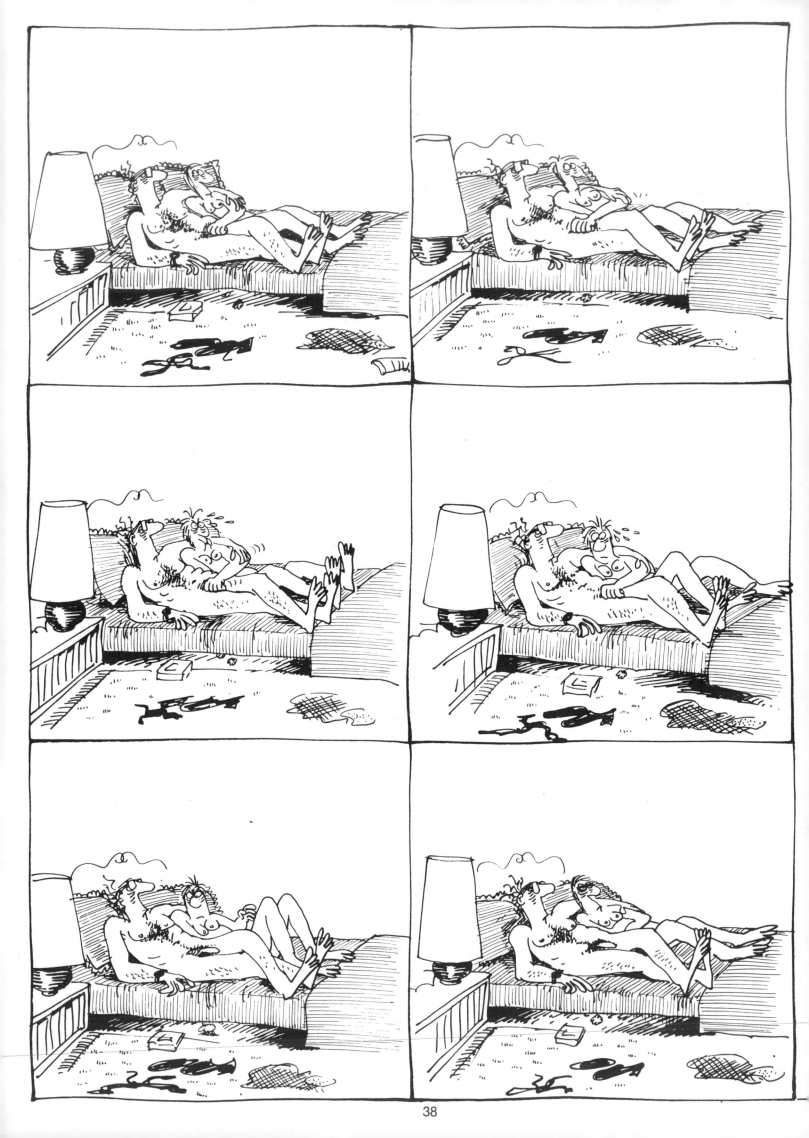

CHAPTER XXXIV

* THE LOVER *

I always loved women and believe myself loved by them semi-colon

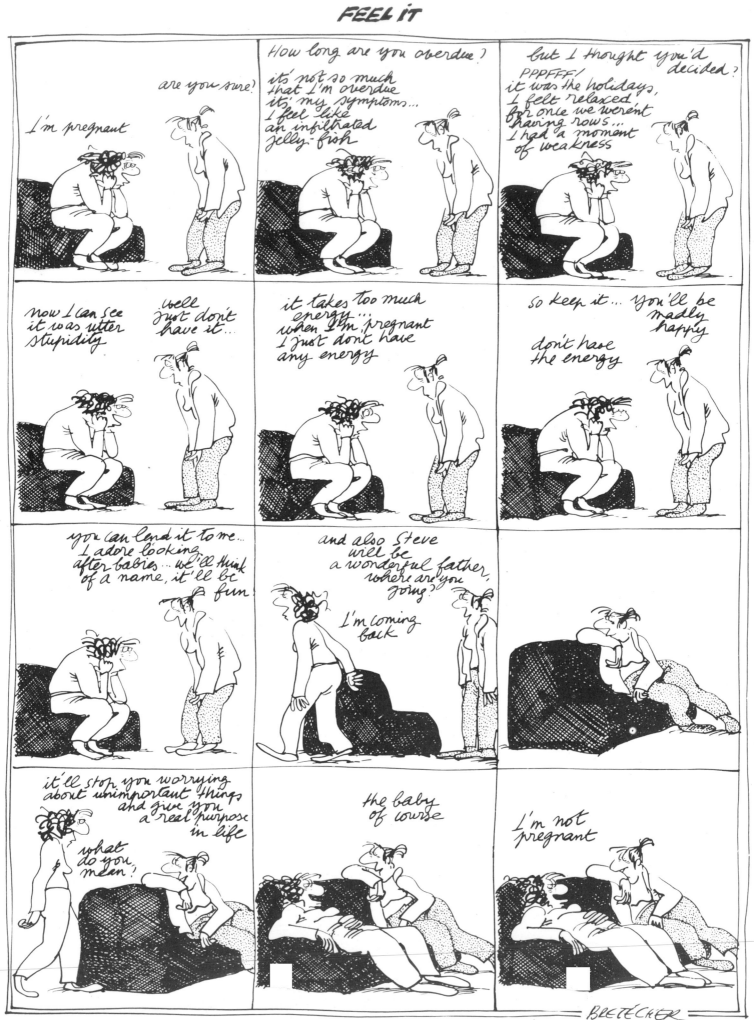

EYES HAVE IT

SUMMER UNIFORM

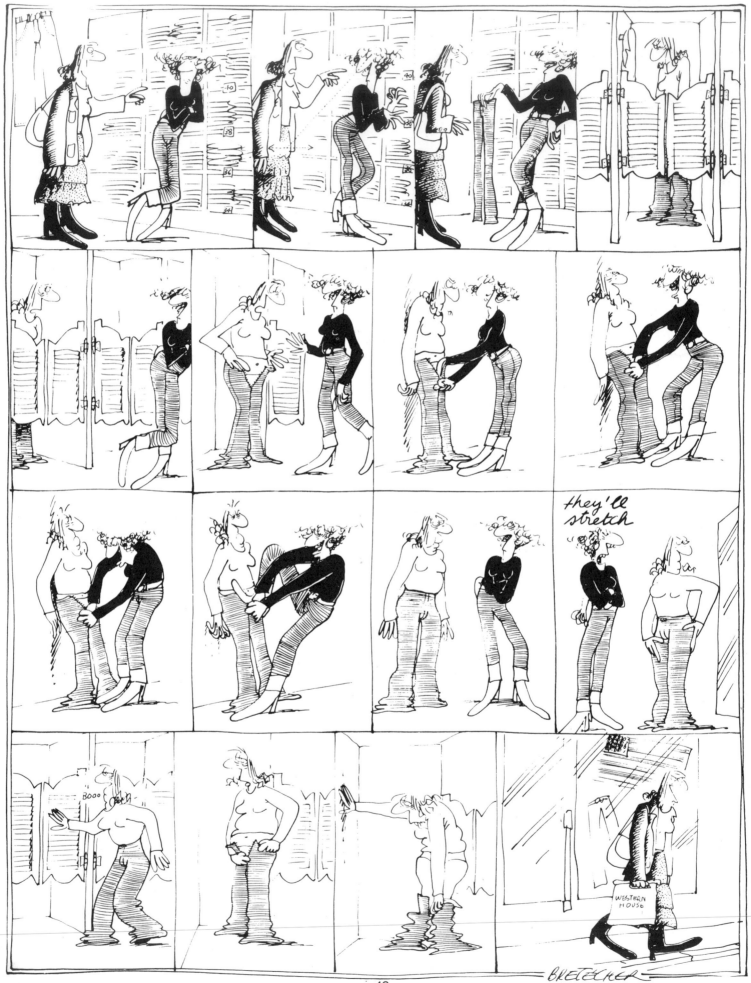

ROMANTICA

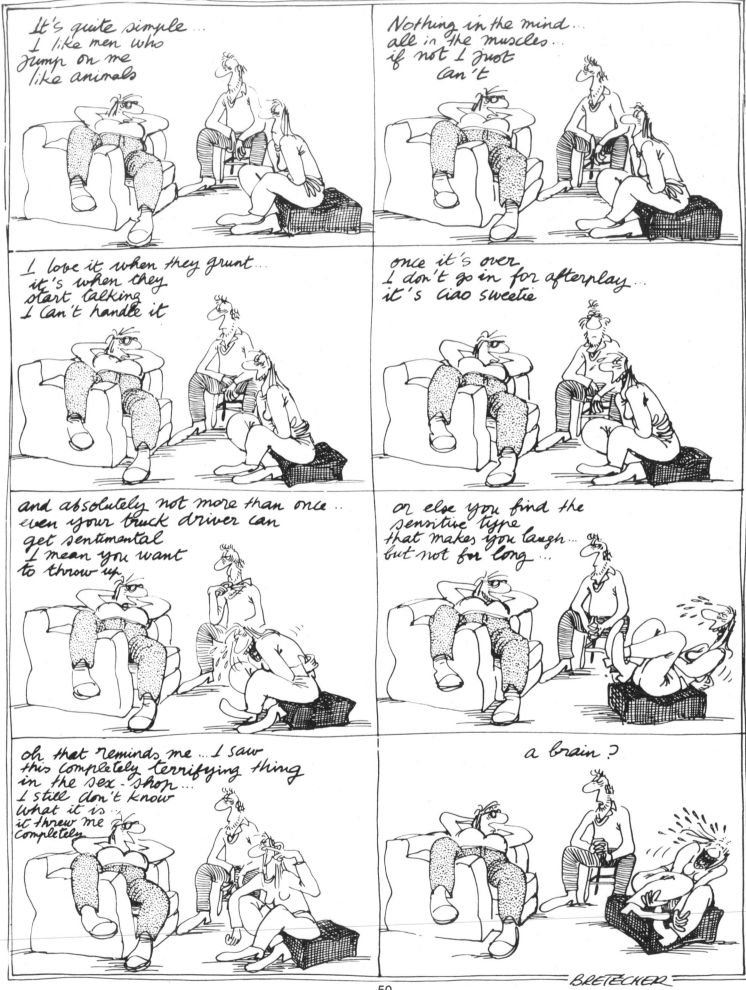

ANGRY YOUNG MAN

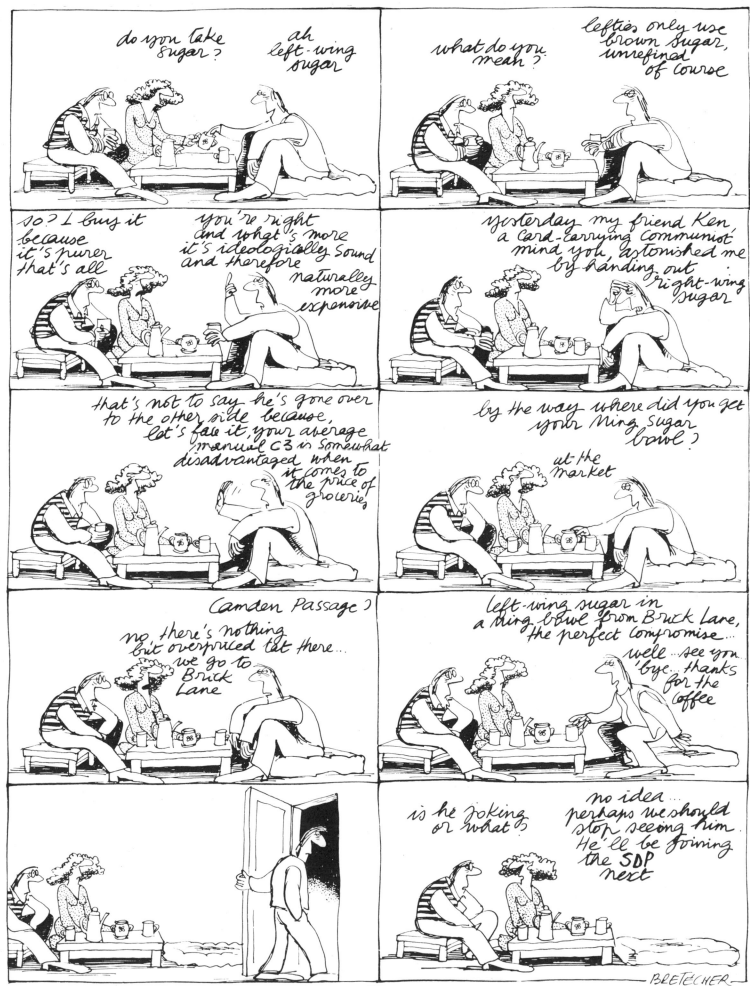

COMMON PROGRAMME

THE NEW MAN

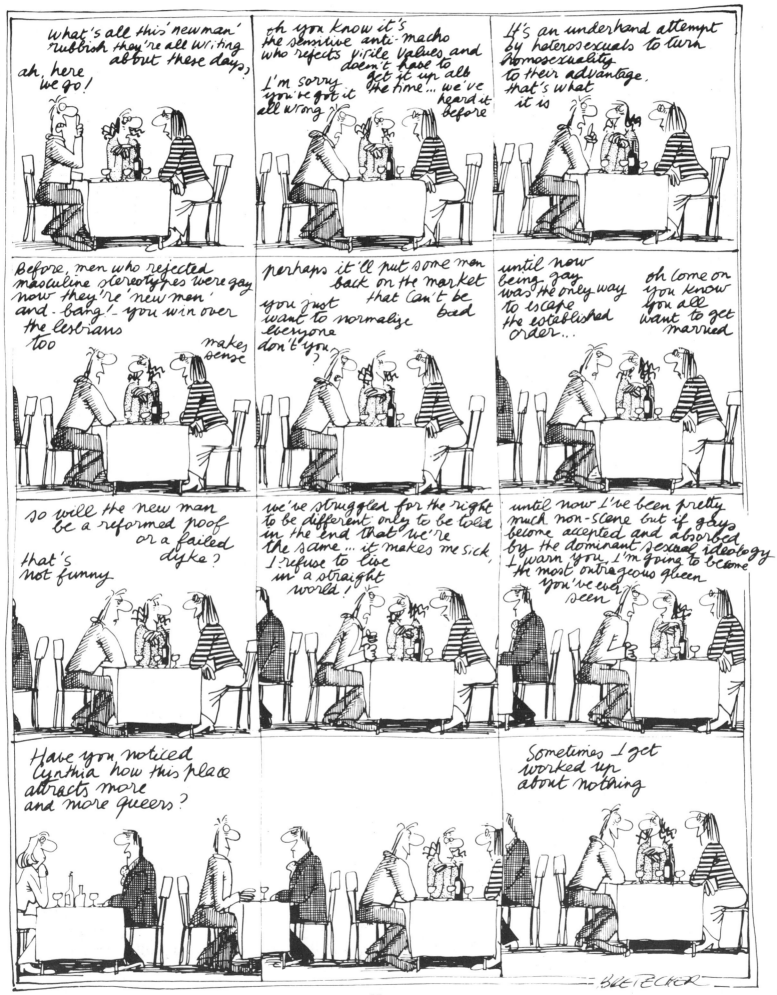

SOCIAL CONSCIENCE

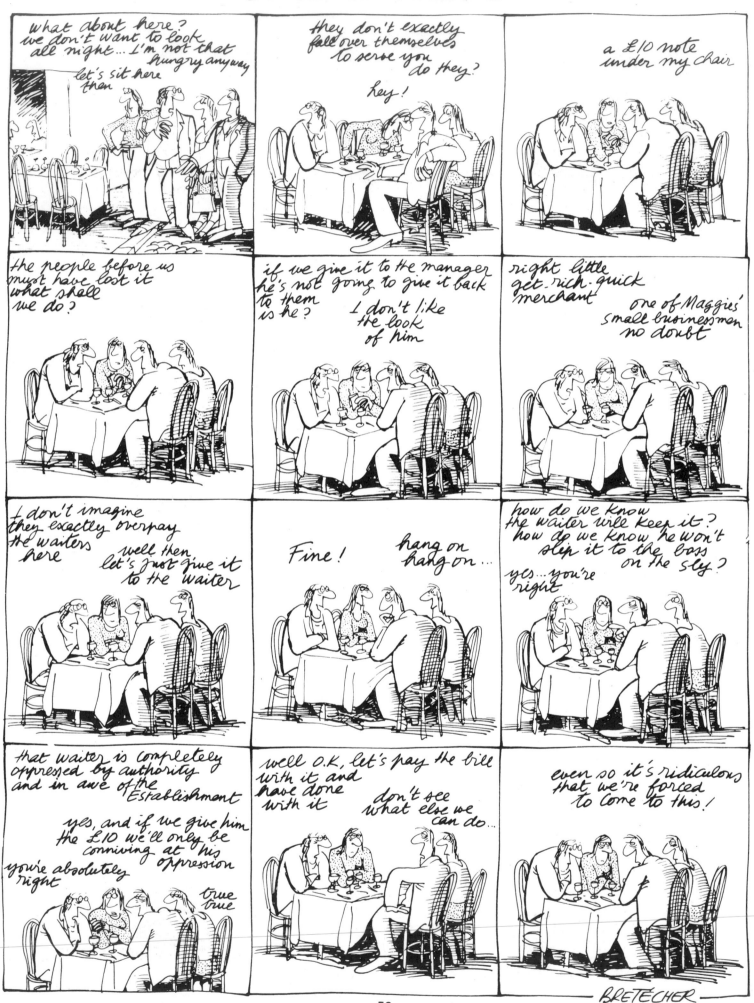

lady luck

POLYGAMY

where there's life

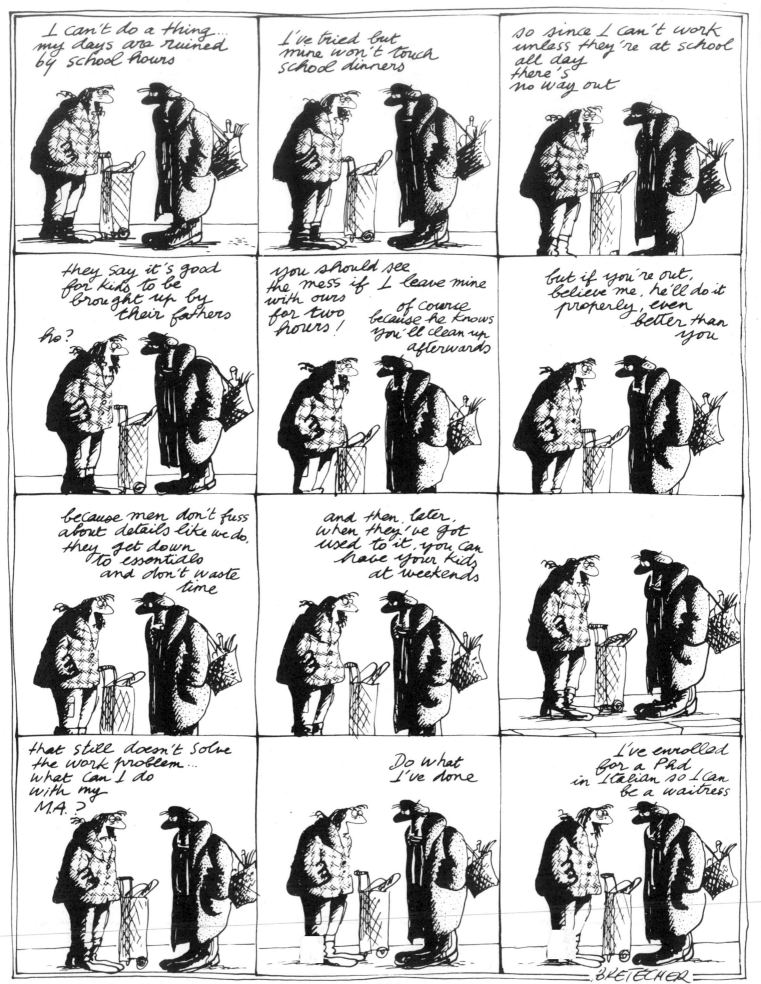

INGRATITUDE